Y0-BCM-934

Fanny Elssler's Cachucha

Fanny Elssler in the Cachucha
Lithograph by C. Motte from a drawing by
Achille Deveria

FANNY ELSSLER'S CACHUCHA

Transcribed from the original Zorn notation by
ANN HUTCHINSON

Styled by
FELISA VICTORIA

THEATRE ARTS BOOKS
New York

First published 1981
by arrangement with Dance Books Ltd
THEATRE ARTS BOOKS
153 Waverly Place
New York, N.Y. 10014

ISBN 0–87830–575–0

© *1981 by Ann Hutchinson Guest*

Contents

Credits

This book would not have come into being but for a series of events. I wish therefore to give special thanks and appreciation to the following:

To IVOR GUEST for giving me the Zorn book containing the Cachucha.

To PETER BRINSON for providing the incentive to revive the work by including it in his programme "The World of Giselle", performed by his educational touring company, Ballet For All.

To FELISA VICTORIA for contributing definitive information concerning the steps and providing styling, particularly for the arms.

To PHILIPPA HEALE for the first trial edition of the Cachucha score.

To IRENE POLITIS for her beautiful autography of the final Labanotation version.

Fanny Elssler's Cachucha

Its Significance and Its Preservation

by IVOR GUEST

FEW DANCES have created such a furore in their time, or assumed such significance in the context of the artistic development of ballet, as the *Cachucha,* which even today is indelibly associated with the name of the ballerina who first performed it. That ballerina was Fanny Elssler, one of the key figures in the great renaissance of ballet that was stimulated by the ideals and moods of Romanticism in the first half of the nineteenth century.[1]

The *Cachucha* also marked the moment when Fanny Elssler attained maturity as an artist. She was twenty-six when she first danced it, having been born in the outskirts of Vienna in 1810. She came from a family with a strong musical tradition, her father and his father before him having served the composer Haydn as valet and amanuensis. Following in the footsteps of two of her sisters, she entered the ballet of the Vienna Opera as a child, gaining her first stage experience at an unusually early age. Her exceptional talent was quickly recognised, and soon her services were in demand beyond the frontiers of her native Austria: first in Naples, then successively in Berlin, London, and – what in those days was the ultimate testing ground for a ballerina – Paris. Dr. Louis Véron, the director of the Paris Opéra, had merely seen her as a counter-attraction to his established star, Marie Taglioni. He did not realise the profound significance of the contribution she was to make to the development of the Romantic ballet – how she was to complement the older ballerina by bringing out a totally contrasting facet of Romanticism. That was only to become evident when she presented her *Cachucha* two years after her début at the Opéra.

In the *Cachucha* she expressed to perfection the earthly, exotic quality of Romanticism, which had its counterparts, in other fields of art, in Delacroix's *Death of Sardanapalus,* the polonaises of Chopin, and Gautier's *Voyage en Espagne.* This formed a most striking contrast to the poetic mood that Taglioni caught so magically in her dancing. It was now recognised that in the field of ballet there were two very different styles that at the same time opposed and complemented one another: the *danse ballonnée* with which Taglioni conveyed the mystery of ethereal spirits flitting weightlessly in dreamy moonlit landscapes, and the *danse tacquetée* which was Elssler's forte, a style much more closely bound to the boards, as its name implied, and lending itself to the exploitation of delicate *pointe* work on the one hand and the performance of stylised national dances on the other. The *Cachucha* established the dichotomy that was the strength of the Romantic ballet; it revealed the range of expression that could stretch from a passionate Spanish dancer to the insubstantial spirit of a forest glade, and inspired Théophile

11

Gautier's oft-quoted comparison of Taglioni and Elssler as the Christian dancer and the pagan dancer.

The *Cachucha* was interpolated in Act II, Scene IV of Jean Coralli's ballet-pantomime, *Le Diable boiteux,* which was first performed at the Paris Opéra on June 1st, 1836. This ballet was based on the well-known novel of the same name by Le Sage. Its hero, the student Cleophas, frees the limping devil Asmodeus from the bottle in which he has been imprisoned, and as a reward, is introduced, one after another, to the three women who have caught his fancy at a ball. One of these is the Spanish Dancer, Florine (the role played by Elssler), who has given him a rose. After declaring his love for her, Cleophas is taken up on to the rooftops, and from there is enabled, through Asmodeus's magic, to look down into Florine's salon. She has invited some of her admirers to supper, and enflames their passions by dancing the *Cachucha,* with all its flirtatious overtones, before them. Cleophas realises how fickle she is, and as she ends the dance, he throws her rose down at her feet.

The scene in Coralli's ballet *Le Diable boiteux* in which Fanny Elssler first performed the Cachucha at the Paris Opéra in 1836. Engraving by Timms from a drawing by Jules Collignon (*Les Beautés de l'Opéra,* Paris, 1845).

This was one of many dramatic moments in the ballet, which threw into relief Elssler's dramatic gifts as never before. But what remained most vividly in the audience's memories afterwards was the *Cachucha,* a dance full of "effective moments, bold thrusting movements and graceful poses."[2] Fanny Elssler was to dance it regularly, as an isolated number, throughout the rest of her career, from her native Vienna to London, from the stages of North America and the great Tacon opera house of Havana to the Imperial Theatres of St. Petersburg and Moscow. Such was the sensation it caused that, whenever and wherever she was engaged, it was unthinkable for her not to perform it. Not only that, but imitators danced it in the most out-of-the-way places which were off the route of her extensive travels: a playbill in the Harvard Theatre Collection records that a Mrs. Leach was dancing it with a Mr. Rivers at the New Theatre, Calcutta, in 1841.

In arranging this dance herself, Fanny had based it on an authentic model. Spanish dancing had acquired a considerable vogue in Paris since the arrival, early in 1834, of four celebrated dancers from Madrid, Dolores Serral, Manuela Dubinon, Francisco Font and Mariano Camprubì. Until then few Spanish dancers had been seen outside Spain, and it was only political considerations that brought them to Paris, the theatres of Madrid having been closed as a result of a dynastic crisis and these four dancers being exceptionally authorised to accept a foreign engagement. They danced in the classical Spanish style which had been developed towards the end of the eighteenth century. Their technique comprised elements taken from ballet, such as *entrechats* and even *pistolets,* and included in their repertory were *boleros, seguidillas manchegas,* the *corraleras sevillanas,* the *fandango,* the *zapateado* . . . and the *cachucha.*

Unlike the *bolero,* which is in 3/4 time, the *cachucha* was danced to a melody – the same which Fanny Elssler was to use – in 3/8, and in common with most Spanish classical dances, the score was divided into three *coplas,* each comprising three *veces,* or variations of steps. There was a variety of *bolero* called the *bolero con cachucha,* in which, as its name implies, passages of the *cachucha* were sandwiched in with the *bolero,* and the *cachucha* also found a place in the *seguidillas taleadas,* which was said to be a combination of the original *seguidilla* with the *cachucha.*

In his *Notes upon Dancing,* published in 1847, Carlo Blasis described the *cachucha* in these words: "The name of this dance is a word in very general signification, and is applied to an infinite number of articles, by way perhaps of abbreviation, as caps, fans, &c. The *Cachucha Solo* is danced either by a man or a woman alone, though better suited to the latter, and is admirably calculated for and adapted to that melody of music by which it is always accompanied, and which is sometimes calm and graceful, at others sprightly and vivacious, and sometimes impassioned and expressive."[3]

Fanny would have seen these Spanish dancers perform on several occasions, both in Paris and in London, and since no other Spanish dancers of note were appearing in either capital at that time, one or other of them must have provided her with the inspiration for her famous *Cachucha.* It is reasonable to assume, too, that she grasped at the opportunity to study the elements of Spanish classical dancing under one of these celebrated exponents and to learn some of the dances of their country.

In the stylised version which she herself performed Fanny was at her most fascinating and had all the *jeunesse dorée* of Paris at her feet. In a short time the general public echoed this adulation, and the *Cachucha* made history at the Paris Opéra by having to be encored almost at every performance. Charles de Boigne in his *Petits Mémoires de l'Opéra* described how the public was gradually won over. "The real public," he wrote, "needed several performances to become accustomed to the *Cachucha.* The contortions, the movements of the hips, the provocative gestures, the arms which seem to seek and embrace an absent lover, the mouth crying out for a kiss, the thrilling, quivering, twisting body, the captivating music, the castanets, the strange costume, the shortened skirt, the low-cut, half-open bodice, and withal all Elssler's sensual grace, lascivious abandon and plastic beauty were very much appreciated by the opera-glasses of the orchestra stalls and the side boxes. The public, the real public, found it more difficult to accept those choreographic audacities, those exaggerated looks, and it can be said that it was the *loges infernales* which forced the success on this occasion. The French *Cachucha* is not a natural, inborn taste; it is an acquired taste."[4]

Théophile Gautier was among the first to declare his enthusiasm. There was no more fervent *Hispanophil* than he, but when he visited Spain in 1840 he never found a dancer to match Fanny Elssler. "I have seen Rosita Diaz, Lola and the finest dancers of Madrid, Seville, Cadiz and

A moment from Fanny Elssler's Cachucha – *le rhombe-montant* – caught by the artist Franz Seitz. (F. Löhle, *Theater-Catechismus*, Munich, n.d.)

Granada," he declared. "I have seen the *gitanas* in Albaicin, but nothing approaches that *Cachucha* as danced by Fanny Elssler."[5]

Fanny Elssler's *Cachucha* also fired the imagination of artists. Lithographs depicted her in poses from the dance, and the sculptor, Jean-Auguste Barre, made a "ravishing" statuette of her. The dance was parodied in the smaller theatres, and was even presented on horseback at the circus. It was selected as one of the themes for the decoration of a popular dance hall, and when some Spanish dancers arrived to perform the "authentic *Cachucha*," critics rose hotly to defend Fanny's version.

Gautier's description of Fanny Elssler in the *Cachucha* finds its place in most anthologies of the dance. "She comes forward," he wrote, "in a basquine skirt of pink satin trimmed with wide flounces of black lace; her skirt, weighted at the hem, fits tightly on the hips; her wasp–like figure is boldly arched back, making the diamond brooch on her bodice sparkle; her leg, smooth as marble, gleams through the fine mesh of her silk stocking; and her small foot, now still, only awaits the signal from the orchestra to burst into action. How charming she is, with her high comb, the rose at her ear, the fire in her eyes and her sparkling smile! At the tips of her rosy fingers the ebony castanets are aquiver. Now she springs forward and the resonant clatter of her castanets breaks out; she seems to shake down clusters of rhythm with her hands. How she twists! How she bends! What fire! What voluptuousness! What ardour! Her swooning arms flutter about her drooping head, her body curves back, her white shoulders almost brush the floor. What a charming moment! Would you not say that in that hand, as it skims over the dazzling barrier of the footlights, she is gathering up all the desires and all the enthusiasm of the audience?"[6]

A more prosaic account of the dance was given by the Danish choreographer, August Bournonville, in his memoirs. Considering the fluency of his pen, in fact, it is disappointingly brief. "The dance begins," he described, "with a graceful advance, and then a few steps back. She performed the first part as if she meant to say, 'Be content with a little jest'; but in the second portion a rapturous glow suffused her entire countenance, which radiated a halo of joy. This moment never failed to have its effect, and from then on the whole dance became a frolic in which she drove her audience wild with delight."[7]

Apart from Pauline Duvernay, who in 1837 was the first to dance the *Cachucha* in London when *Le Diable boiteux* was revived there, no other ballerina of note dared risk comparison with Elssler in her most famous dance. She herself danced it regularly all over the Western world until her retirement in 1851, and its magic lingered long in the memory of those who had seen it.

Fanny Elssler lived in comfortable retirement for many years and died in 1884. Some years before her death Eduard Hanslick, the music critic, was present at a soirée when the subject of the *Cachucha* was raised. After some of the older guests had tried to describe it, one of the younger men begged Fanny to give those who had never had the good fortune of seeing her dance it an idea of her art. At first, with charming modesty, she tried to decline, but her hostess added her plea and she rose from her chair.

"She asked me to go to the piano," wrote Hanslick, "and indicated to me the tempo of the *Cachucha,* which she took much more slowly than usual. It was lucky for me that this simple music was so easy to play, for in order not to lose one of Fanny's movements, I was obliged to play with my head turned away from the piano. It was an unforgettable sight. Fanny Elssler had tucked up her dress a little. Two or three times she went up and down the vast room dancing, or rather drifting, with such graceful and expressive inclinations of her head and body and such rounded and undulating movements of her arms, that I understood for the first time the meaning of the ideal dance. All our ballerinas dance only with their legs."[8]

The contemporary descriptions, for all their vivid imagery, give no precise indications of the dance as it was actually set and performed by Fanny Elssler, and no other ballerina took it into her repertory after she retired. It would then, no doubt, have been forgotten and irretrievably lost had it not been for a little known dance teacher who had settled far away in the Black Sea port of Odessa. This man, Friedrich Albert Zorn, was also something of a scholar. Absorbed by the challenge of producing an accurate record of dance movements, he worked out a system of notation, inspired by that of Saint-Léon, which he used to illustrate his technical manual on the dance. In this book, by a happy chance, he included the *Cachucha* as an example of his system, and it is from this record that the *Cachucha* has been revived in recent years.

Two questions have to be faced. Did Zorn write down the dance as Elssler performed it, and if so, how accurate is his record? The evidence is circumstantial, but it is convincing. Unfortunately Zorn did not state, in so many words, that what he had written down was

15

Elssler's version, although he mentions Elssler specifically in the accompanying text as having established its popularity. From what we know about Zorn himself, however, it would be perverse not to accept that he had recorded an authentic version of the dance. A study of his book reveals at once how conscious he was of the historical development of the various dances of his time. He was not a creative spirit, but a scholarly researcher, and the assumption must be made that he based his version of the *Cachucha* on the performances of this dance which he himself had seen. When and where, then, could he have seen it? We know that he spent more than a year in Paris at the time that Elssler was dancing it at the Opéra, and his discovery of this dance must therefore relate back to her own stirring rendering, for there was virtually no one else whom he could have seen perform it either then or later. The only other ballerina of consequence who danced it was Pauline Duvernay, who did so in London (which we have no evidence of his having visited) and, in any event, probably in the same version as Elssler. There is no evidence either that Zorn ever visited Spain, and if he had, he would have recorded the *Cachucha* in a less choreographically formalised form and also, in all probability, as a dance for a couple. The conclusion must therefore be drawn that his original source was Fanny Elssler's performance.

The notation of the *Cachucha* that appears in Zorn's book in 1887 would have been made many years after he had seen Elssler dance it, but it must have been based on earlier notes, probably a verbal description, which he made when his memory was fresh. The comparative simplicity of the steps and their frequent repetition makes recording the dance easy enough.

Like any dance that is handed down, details are changed and little subtleties are inevitably lost, but we can safely assume that the record that Zorn has left us brings us into contact with the performance of Fanny Elssler nearly a century and a half ago. Her personal artistry, which clothed the dance with a magic that no words or symbols can describe, can now only be imagined, but the framework of the *Cachucha* is preserved as a memorial to the great artist for whom it was created and – let us not forget – to the bespectacled old dancing master who recorded it.

NOTES

[1] For Fanny Elssler generally, see the writer's biography of her, *Fanny Elssler* (London & Middletown, Conn., 1970), and for the impact of Romanticism on ballet, see Chapter 1 of his *Romantic Ballet in Paris* (2nd edition, London, 1980).

[2] Castil-Blaze, *L'Académie Impériale de Musique* (Paris, 1855), vol. II, p. 251.

[3] Carlo Blasis, *Notes upon Dancing, Theoretical and Practical* (London, 1847), p. 51.

[4] Charles de Boigne, *Petits Mémoires de l'Opéra* (Paris, 1857), p. 132.

[5] Théophile Gautier et al., *Les Beautés de l'Opéra* (Paris, 1845), notice of *Le Diable boiteux*, p. 21.

[6] Théophile Gautier et al., op. cit., pp. 20-21.

[7] August Bournonville, *Mit Theaterliv* (Copenhagen, 1848), vol. I, p. 77. Translation by Patricia McAndrew, *My Theatre Life* (London & Middletown, Conn., 1979), p. 49.

[8] Eduard Hanslick, *Aus meinem Leben (Deutsche Rundschau*, vol. 77, 1893, p. 214).

The Story of the Cachucha Revived

by ANN HUTCHINSON

In 1966, as an engagement anniversary present, my husband, Ivor Guest, gave me a copy of the 1905 edition of Zorn's book "Grammar of the Art of Dancing". Having studied the Zorn dance notation system at the New York Public Library years before, I was delighted at last to have a copy of my own. "It has the Cachucha at the end," Ivor, who was at that time writing his biography of Fanny Elssler, told me, "You ought to reconstruct it sometime." When he mentioned this possibility casually to Peter Brinson, Brinson saw it as an exciting addition to the programme "The World of Giselle" which he was preparing for his educational touring company, Ballet For All. The Cachucha would provide the means of introducing Elssler and demonstrating the contrast with the ethereal style of Taglioni. With this incentive and a deadline of the first performance set for September, 1967, I took the book with me on our Easter holiday in Crete and transcribed the notation sitting in the sun amid the spring flowers at Knossos. Back in England, with the music taped, I tried out the steps. How awkward many of them were.* Despite the seemingly simple notation and the word notes many passages were unclear. I had made a verbatim transcription from the Zorn notation into Labanotation and the resulting "spelling" of the movements was often static and uncomfortable. Sometimes insufficient information was given, elsewhere there was too much fussy overdetailed description which did not help. Happily at hand was Felisa Victoria, the Spanish dance specialist who became fascinated by the project and recognized many of the steps as belonging to the technique of the classic Spanish dance. We realized, however, that Fanny Elssler's dance would have been a somewhat balleticized version since she had not trained specifically in Spanish dance, nor had she ever visited Spain. Madame Victoria was able to provide subtleties of style which had most probably been present but had not been recorded in the word notes or the notation. For example, arm movements shown by Zorn's stick figures were sparse and static, and we decided that, from the descriptions of the dance by contemporaries, Elssler would have used a more flowing port de bras, such as is common in Spanish dance, and so we incorporated such gestures.

That summer, while in Detroit for the Cecchetti Council of America's summer session, I gave copies of the dance to students of Rose Marie Floyd. By studying the dance ahead they were able to perform it in a demonstration with very few rehearsals. Later that summer, at Jacob's Pillow, I taught it to a gifted student to perform as part of my lecture demonstration. Back in London during August Madame Victoria and I taught the dance to Virginia Wakelyn of the Ballet For All company, the first to give it a professional performance. The original music score of three

---

* See Appendix A for problems met and decisions made.

17

Photo by G. B. L. Wilson

Virginia Wakelyn as Fanny Elssler in the 1967 Ballet for All
production 'The World of Giselle'.

tunes played repeatedly produced a thin and rather dull accompaniment, so John Lanchbery was called upon to make an arrangement for two guitars, two pianos and castanets which provided colour and contrast. From the innate quality of the different steps we provided Lanchbery with suggestions for changes in mood, and this he followed, making the whole dance a delight to perform.

Technically the dance is not difficult to do; the footwork comes fairly easily to a ballet trained dancer, though there are some details which require discipline. It is mainly in the ports de bras that the style is hard to achieve, for dancers fall into the standard ballet positions which are not appropriate. The greatest difficulty is met in performing the many repetitions of the steps, for example the 16 demi-pas de basque advancing towards the audience for which there is a great temptation to change the step, or at least to add some little flourish. It is the mark of a true artist when such repetitions are danced, to stimulate the audience with the repetitions, rather than induce boredom. How this is achieved is up to the artistry of the dancer. We know from contemporary accounts that Fanny possessed tremendous personality and presence and being an exceptional actress, she understood fully the importance of introducing subtle nuances in her dancing. It was with these that she made the Cachucha so special. Nowadays such repetition of dance steps rarely occurs, the audience is showered with an endless change of steps and as a result dancers of today do not learn how to use subtle changes in timing and dynamics in addition to their personal charm to render such repetitions enchanting.

With reprints of the Zorn book making the material much more accessible, others are now trying out the dance, not always, as has been observed, with results which are artistic or accurate. While other interpretations of the Cachucha may be as valid as that produced by myself and Felisa Victoria, we have had several advantages: ample time for the initial translation from the old notation; the opportunity with the tool of Labanotation to work out a score which made kinetic sense; the opportunity to try out the result with many dancers before the final version of

18

the score was set; the chance to go back to the original Zorn and to earlier versions of the Labanotation score for a final check; the use of a fine professional arrangement of the music, and, finally, an authentic costume made for Ballet For All which was an exact replica of an original Elssler costume which Ivor Guest had sketched and measured in the archives in Vienna where it is preserved.

For several years Ballet For All kept the Cachucha in the repertory (Marion Tate for one giving an outstanding performance of it), until Brinson left and concern for historical authenticity declined. The Viennese ballerina, Cristl Zimmerl, who came to London to learn it in preparation for the centenary celebrations in 1969 of the Vienna State Opera, received high acclaim for her performance of it. That same year it was also taught to Merle Park for inclusion in the Royal Academy of Dancing Gala. However, Park did not have enough time to work on it and achieve the fine performance it deserved and so substituted at the last minute a flashy Spanish style dance choreographed for her. This caused Ivor Guest great embarrassment, for it made nonsense of the programme note in which he claimed authenticity for it. At the Academy's assembly in 1972 a most sensitive performance of the dance was given by Margaret Barbieri of the Royal Ballet who not only looked uncannily like Fanny, but intuitively knew how to interpret the various steps and handle the repetitions to produce an enchanting result.

The dream of finally capturing Barbieri's performance on film was realized in the summer of 1980 when Peter Wright, director of Sadler's Wells Royal Ballet was able to schedule special

Photo by Jennie Walton

(*Left*) Cristl Zimmerl performing the Cachucha at the 1969 centenary celebration of the Vienna State Opera. (*Right*) Margaret Barbieri, principal dancer of Sadler's Wells Royal Ballet, performing for the filming of the Cachucha, 1980.

19

rehearsals for her, when Sadler's Wells Theatre itself was available for the filming, as well as Nicholas Morris, director of the Film Division of St. Martin's School of Art. John Lanchbery agreed to our use of the music which he had arranged for the Ballet for All performances, and a new costume was made, designed in every detail to follow the famous lithograph by Achille Deveria.

With the film available, it is now possible for students of dance history and the development of dance styles, as well as students wishing to experience personally the step sequences that Fanny Elssler made so famous, to study it in depth. The film provides an interpretation by a professional dancer, the notation provides the structure of the work with the specific details clearly indicated. Thus has been realized the dream of starting a living library for the dance.

Performance of the Cachucha

Directions for 1967 musical arrangement

Sequence of the dance		Mood and expressive quality
Introduction		
I. 1.	Ballonné Progressif	Gay and light but deliberate.
I. 2.	Pivoter	Quiet and flowing.
I. 3.	Ballonné Rétrograde	Livelier. Definite end.
I. 4.	Frappé, Tortillé	Quiet, teasing step with foot. Definite end.
II. 1.	Le Rhombe en Descendant	Light, slightly faster (step travels around room).
II. 2.	Demi-pas de Basque avec tapés de talons	Start very softly and gradually get louder.
II. 3.	Le Rhombe en Montant	As for II. 1. Definite end.
II. 4.	Tortillé, Pas de Basque Ramassé, Pirouette	With gusto. Definite end.
III. 1.	Ballonné Rétrograde	With more life, fuller (not faster)
III. 2.	Temps de Ciseaux, Pas de Basque, Pivoter	Quieter, but promising things to come
III. 3.	Ballonné, Pirouettes	Stronger, full of life
III. 4.	Ramassé	A little faster, but seductive, build towards end.
IV. 1.	Grand Dégagé	Slower, fuller, more pulled out.
IV. 2.	Dégagé à Genoux	Quite full.
IV. 3.	Ballonnés, Pas Élevés, Révérence	Very gay, teasing, for measures 1-8; 9-16, quieter for big révérence .
Coda	Exit from stage with pas ballonnés and pas élevés.	Final burst of gaiety.

La Cachucha.

Glossary

Springing
For all springs: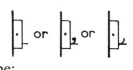

Level of Supports
Ball of foot supports vary in the Zorn drawings and so may be:

Sign for Floor
Floor, (terra): ⊤

Section of Toes
Inside edge:

Representation of the path of the design drawn in the air:

Design Drawing

Indication of the design, the black dot shows the start:

Air design of the ballonné gesture

Performance Notes

Cou-de-pied Foot Position (meas. 1, 2 etc.)

After the ballonné and the step which follows, the cou–de–pied behind should each time be with the foot pointing to the floor (if the figure drawings are to be followed), as in Ex. a). In the score this has been abbreviated to Ex. b):

a)

b)

Torso Bend for Ramassé (meas. 34, etc.)

On the Ramassé the torso should bend sideward as far as the dancer can manage:

The Rhombe (meas. 65-80; 97-112)

In performing both the Rhombe en Descendant and the Rhombe en Montant the body alignment adjusts to keep some contact with the audience, even if this is only suggested by the tilt of the head.

Performance of Arm Movements

It is not clear whether the slight variations in arm positions which occur in the figure drawings are intended or not. We used these variations to add interest to the dance even though, being subtle, they may not be immediately observed.

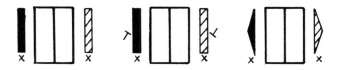

Foot Position for Pirouettes (meas. 3, 162, etc.)

According to the words and the figure drawings, in the retiré position in the pirouette the foot should be pointing down:

Technique of Turning (meas. 17-32)

The footwork described here produces a smooth, fluent turn. Leading with the left shoulder helps initiate the turning.

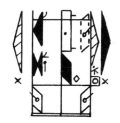

'Lace-making' Step (meas. 49, etc)

The size of the sideward step must be such that the rotating leg finishes with the foot in a perfect 5th position, heel coming to toe:

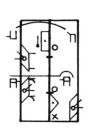

Style for Arms and Body

In the arm positions care should be taken to avoid falling into standard balletic positions. Elbows must be well 'lifted', the arm rotated in one piece, wrists softly curved, not angular. The dance is often vivacious and energetic, but still elegant, not with Flamenco abandon.

23

The Dance

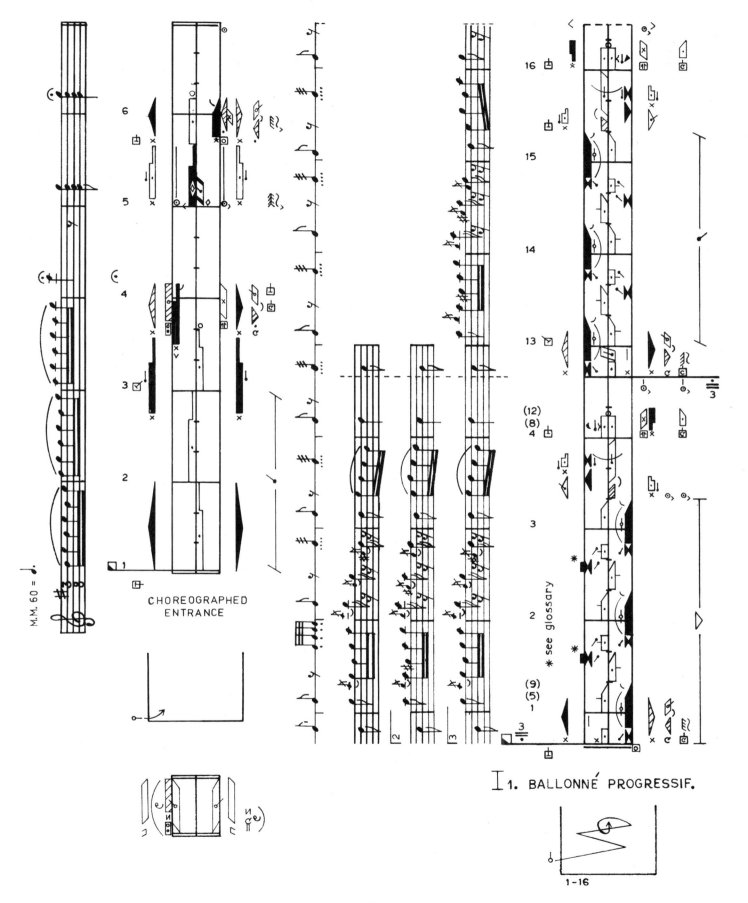

M.M. 60 = ♩.

CHOREOGRAPHED
ENTRANCE

16

15

14

13

(12)
(8)
4

3

2

(9)
(5)
1

* see glossary

I 1. BALLONNÉ PROGRESSIF.

1-16

27

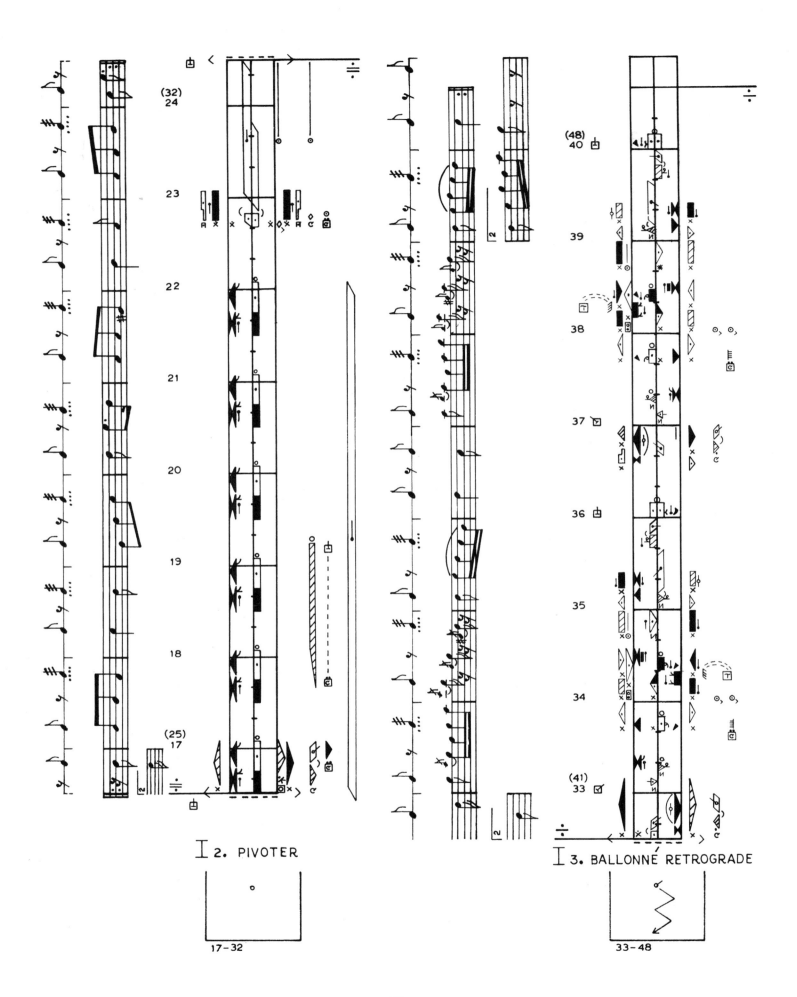

I 2. PIVOTER

17-32

I 3. BALLONNÉ RETROGRADE

33-48

28

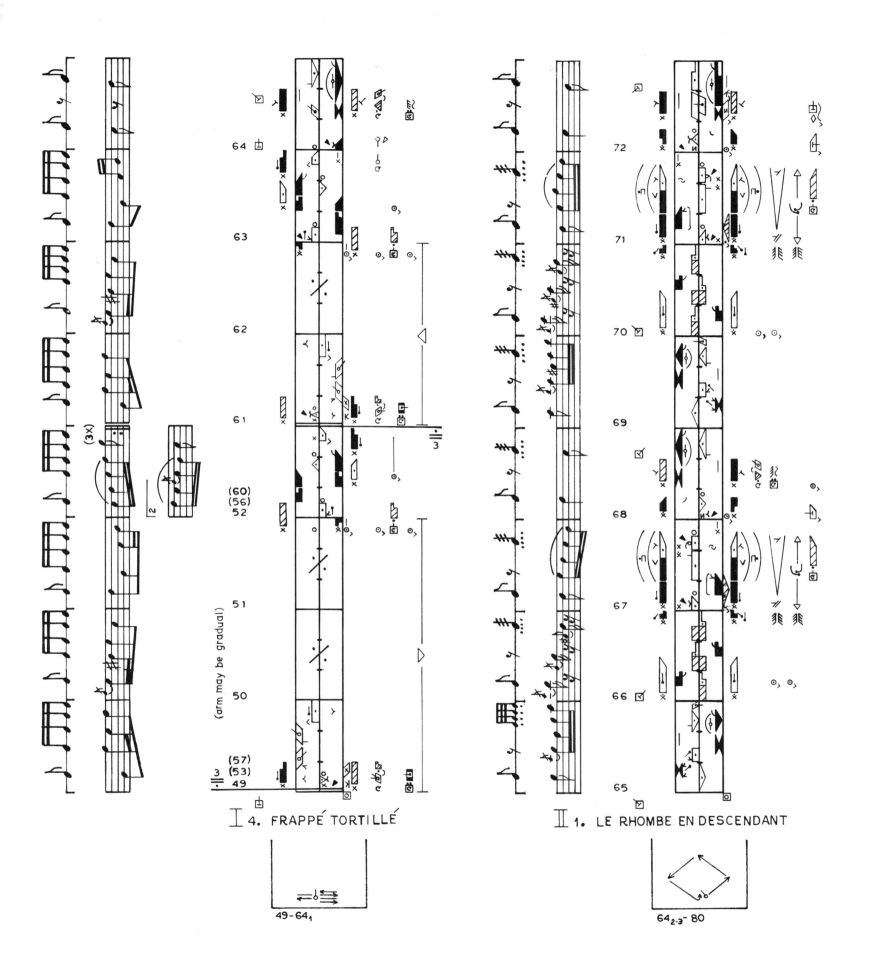

I 4. FRAPPÉ TORTILLÉ

49-64₁

II 1. LE RHOMBE EN DESCENDANT

64₂₋₃ 80

29

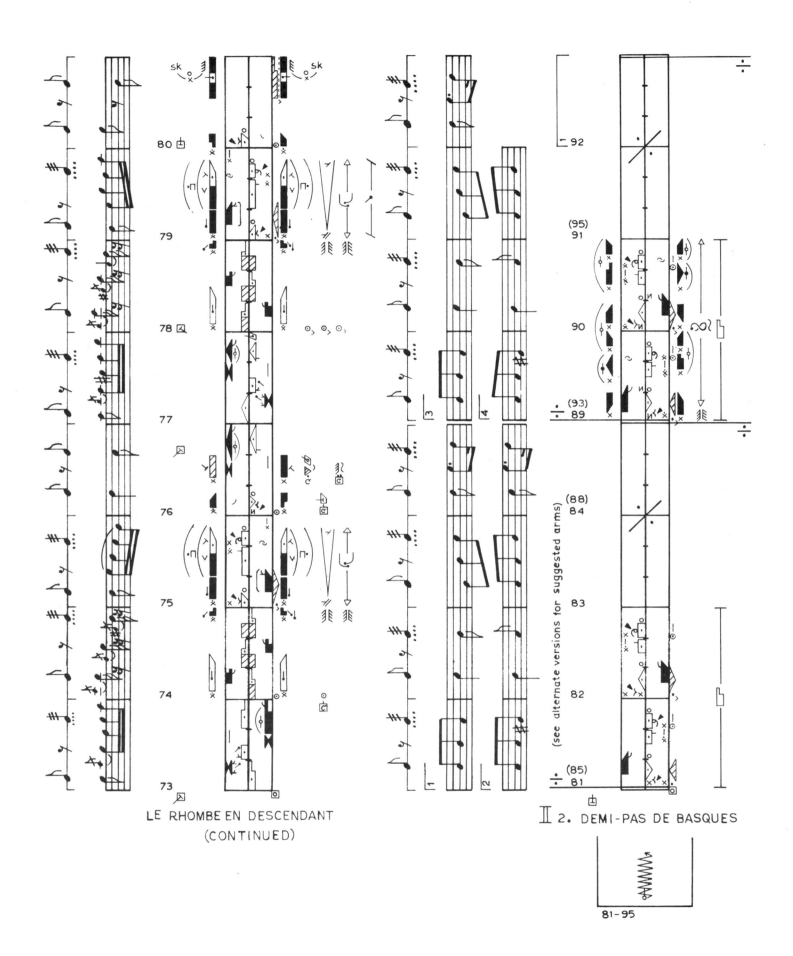

LE RHOMBE EN DESCENDANT
(CONTINUED)

Ⅱ 2. DEMI-PAS DE BASQUES

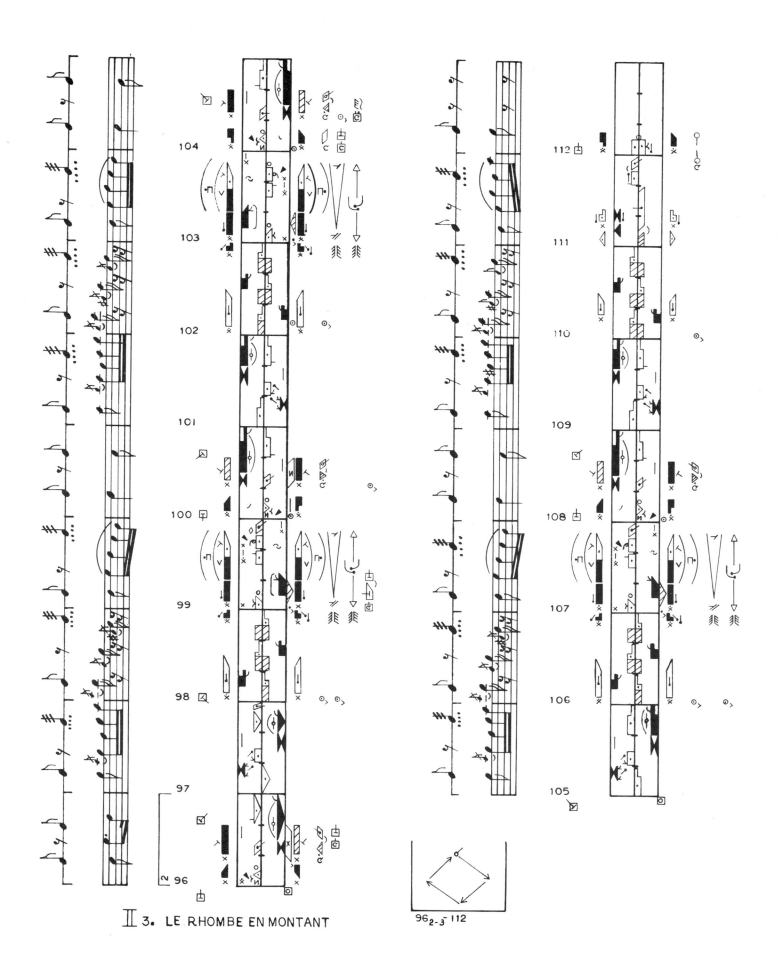

II 3. LE RHOMBE EN MONTANT

96_{2-3} 112

31

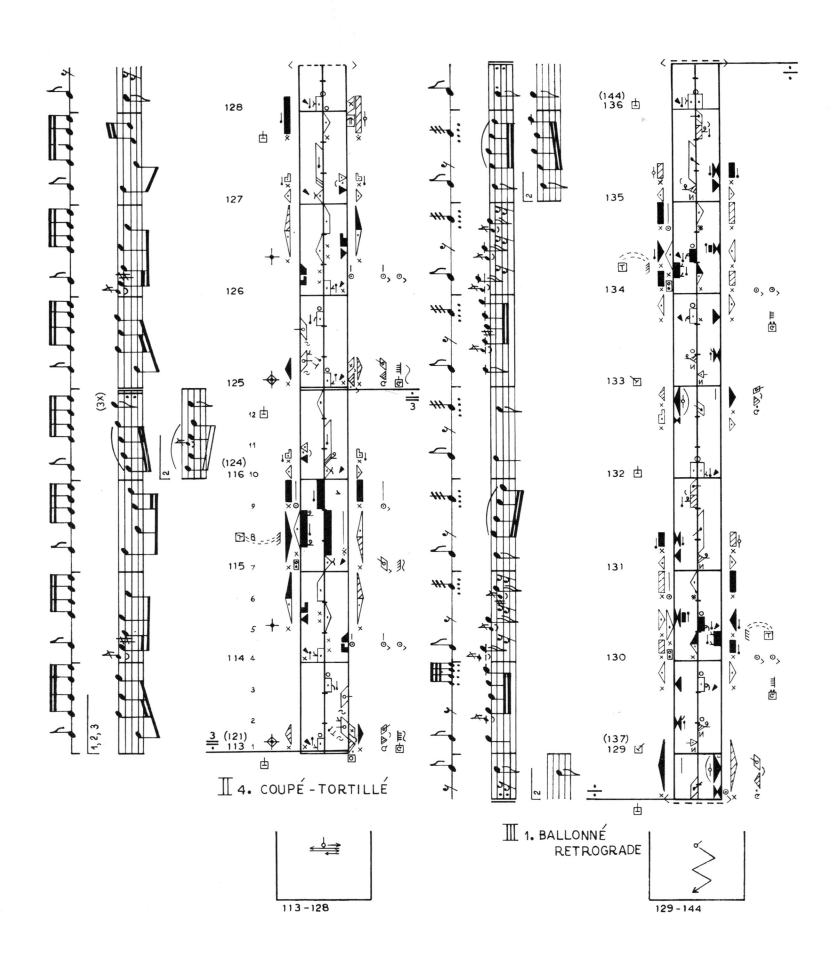

II 4. COUPÉ - TORTILLÉ

III 1. BALLONNÉ
RETROGRADE

113 - 128

129 - 144

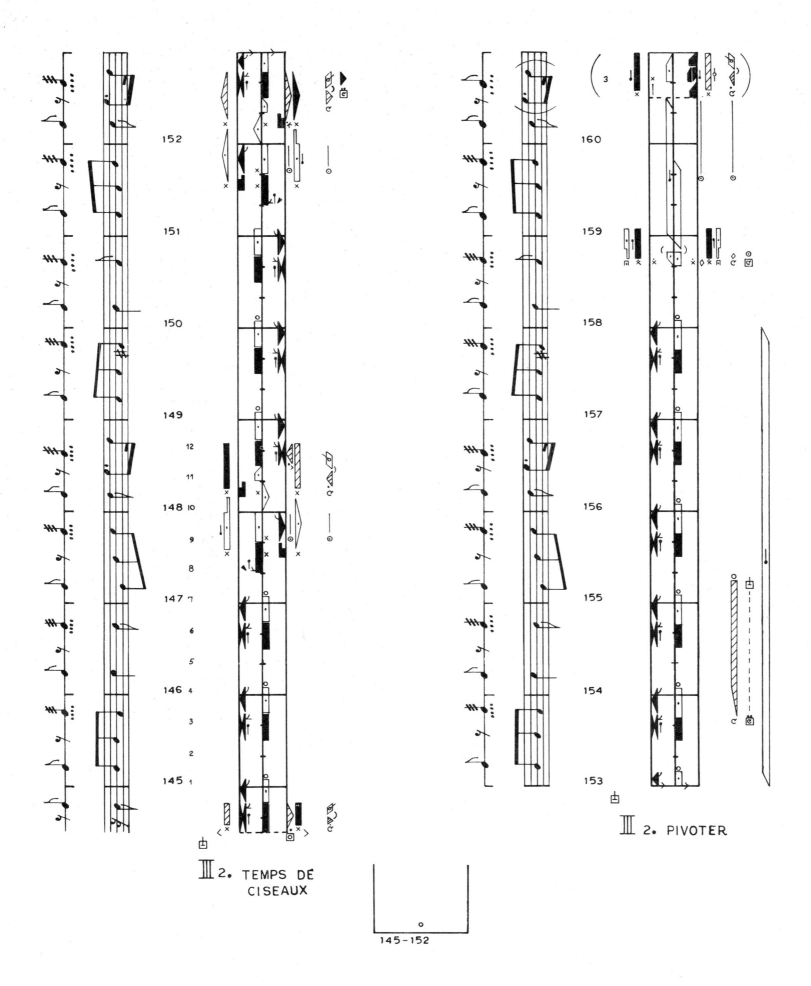

Ⅲ 2. TEMPS DE
CISEAUX

Ⅲ 2. PIVOTER

145-152

33

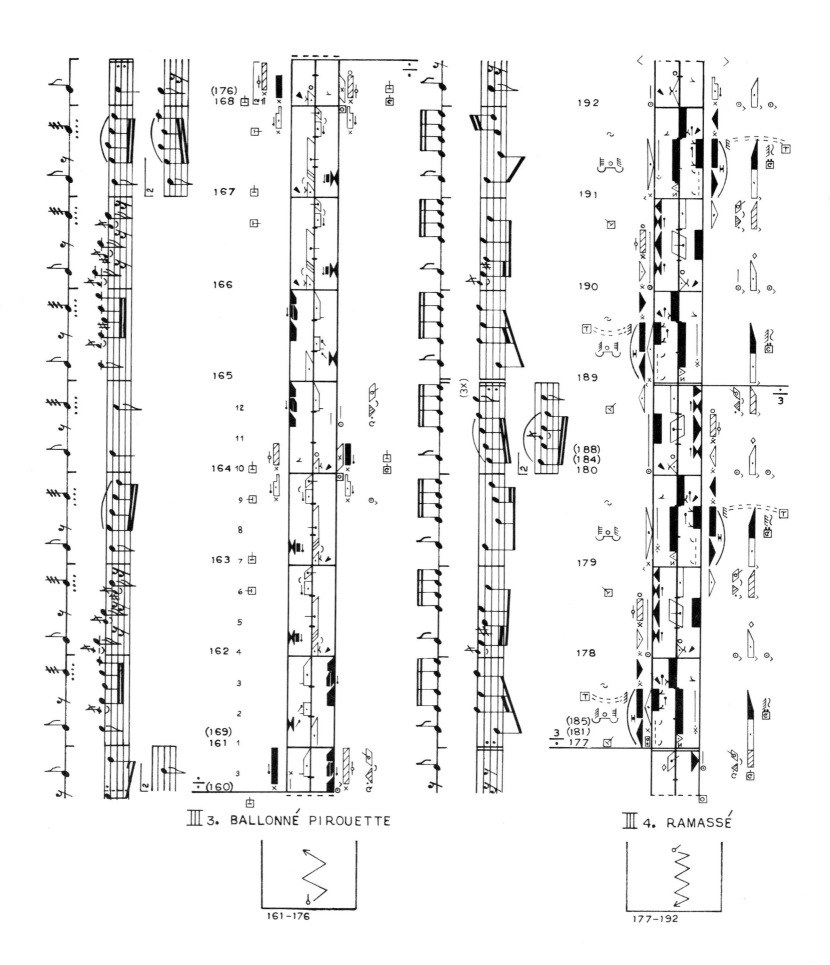

III 3. BALLONNÉ PIROUETTE

161–176

III 4. RAMASSÉ

177–192

34

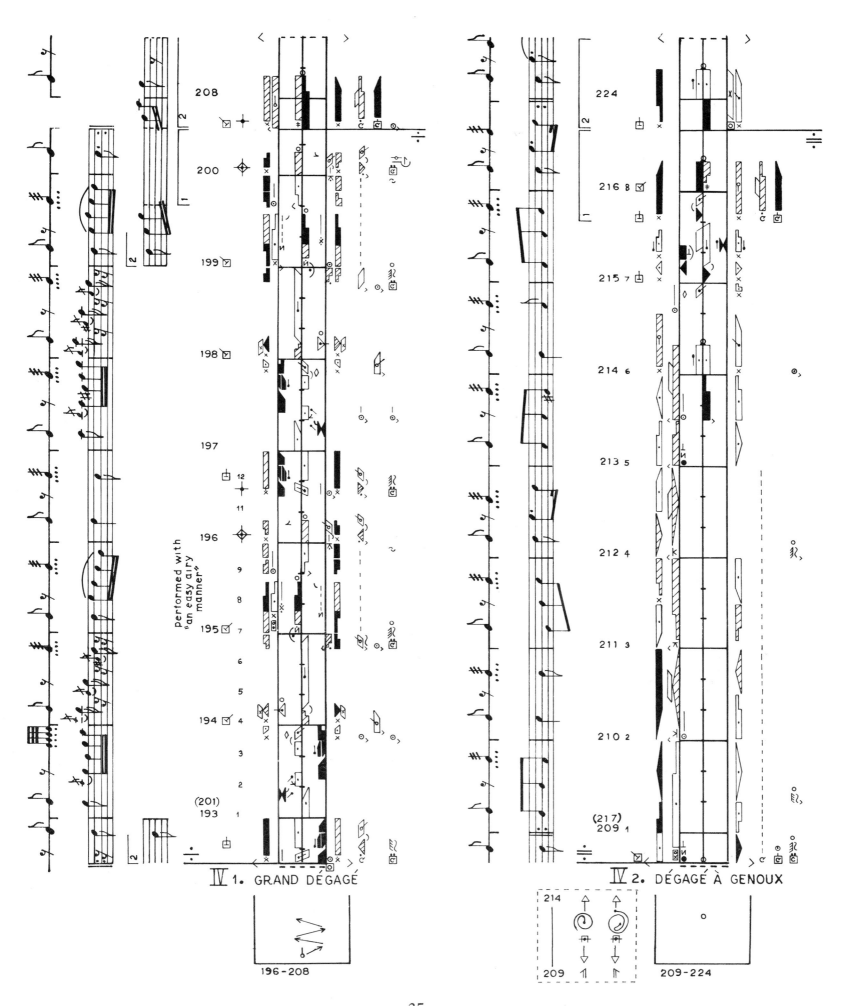

performed with
"an easy airy manner"

IV 1. GRAND DÉGAGÉ

196-208

IV 2. DÉGAGÉ À GENOUX

209-224

35

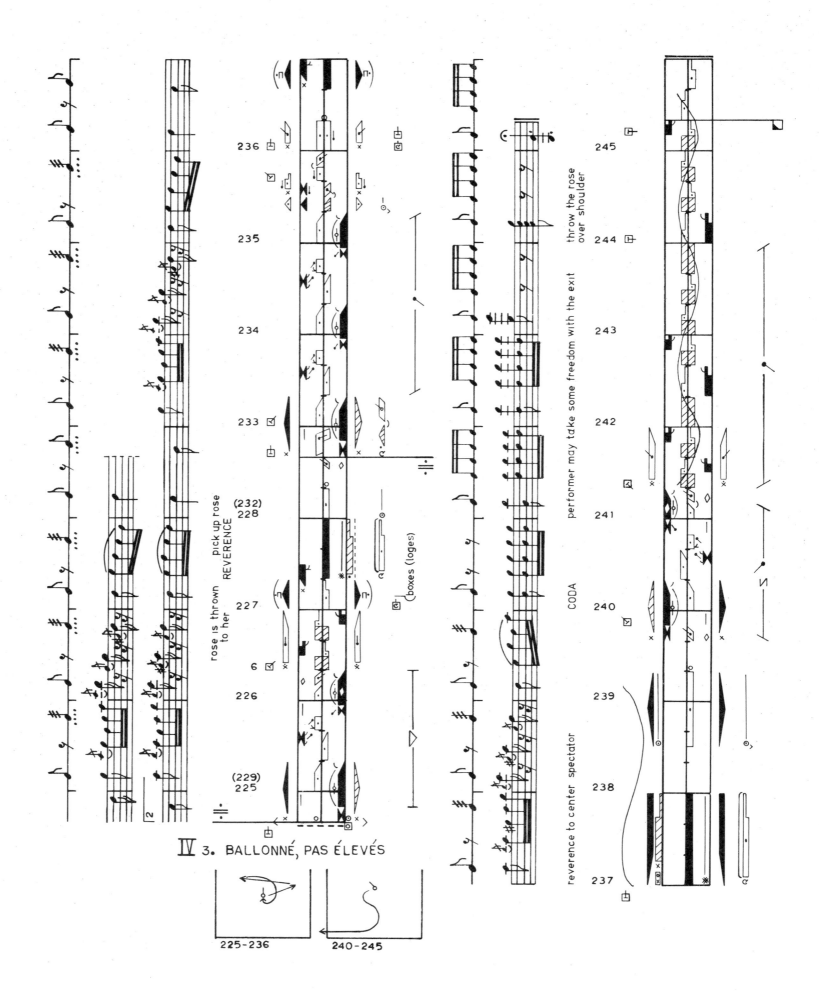

throw the rose over shoulder

performer may take some freedom with the exit

CODA

reverence to center spectator

rose is thrown to her

pick up rose

REVERENCE

(boxes (loges))

236
235
234
233
(232)
228
227
6
226
(229)
225

237
238
239
240
241
242
243
244
245

IV 3. BALLONNÉ, PAS ÉLEVÉS

225-236

240-245

Alternate Versions

The following alternate versions have been tried in the process of solving movement passages that did not work as written or where the need was felt for a minor change or some specific arm movements.

Suggested Arms for the Demi-Pas de Basque:

81-84: hold skirt, small head and body movements.

89-96: figure eight arm pattern increasing in size:

85-88: move skirt side to side:

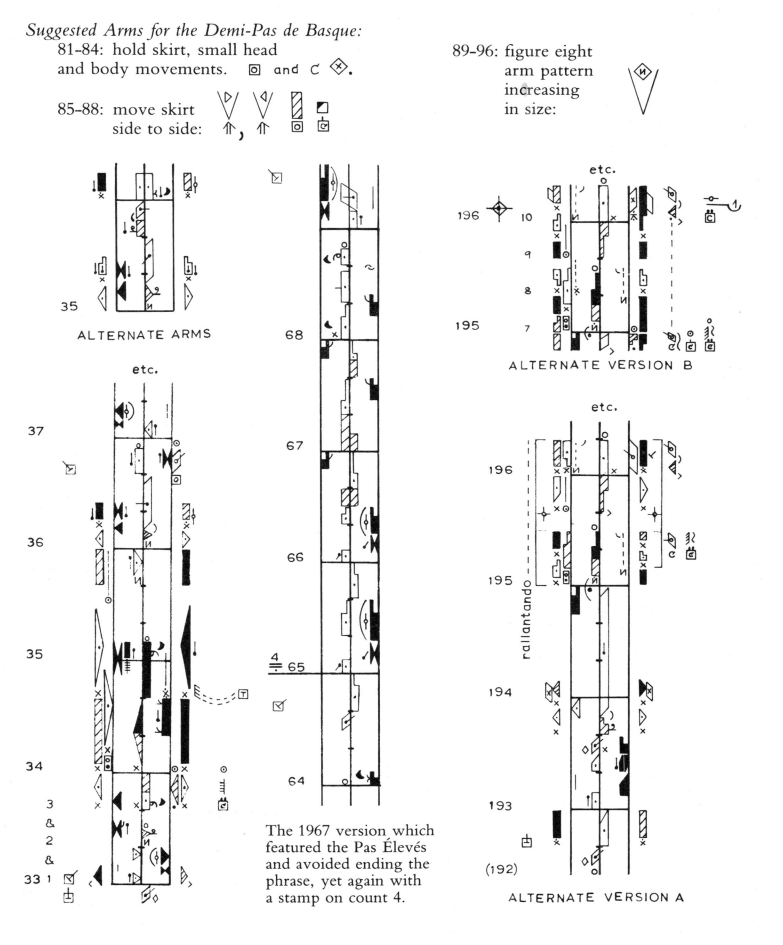

ALTERNATE ARMS

etc.

ALTERNATE VERSION B

The 1967 version which featured the Pas Élevés and avoided ending the phrase, yet again with a stamp on count 4.

ALTERNATE VERSION A

Zorn's Notation and Word Descriptions

(These are reproduced from Zorn's *Grammar of the Art of Dancing,*
Boston, 1905. A reduced facsimile edition is published
by Dance Horizons, New York.)

The Cachucha *(La Cachucha)*

921. The *Cachucha* is a Spanish solo-dance, better adapted for execution by a lady than by a gentleman, which is danced to the melody of an Andalusian national song containing two parts of eight measures each, to which, for the sake of variety, there has been added a third part of similar duration, and the whole is completed by an introduction and a coda.

The celebrated Fanny Elssler, by her wonderful execution, won for this dance a popularity in keeping with its merits.

The word *cachucha*, in Spanish, is a term of endearment, which is applied to particularly attractive or graceful persons or things, and is also used as the name of a certain kind of cap.

922. The music and complete choregraphic description of the Cachucha, which is executed in 3-8 measure, is placed at the top of the succeeding pages.

The clicking of the castanets, which forms so essential a part of the Spanish dances, is generally neglected by all save Spanish dancers. Great care should be devoted to this feature.

It is customary to play a few chords before the regular melody is commenced, as shown in the Music Book (No. 124).

923. The dance is divided into four couplets, and the melody is played four times, ending with the coda.

The script of the first couplet is given upon the first line below the notes, the second on the next, and so on.

Each couplet contains four figures of sixteen measures each, for the third of which the music is the same as for the first.

924. It must not be forgotten that a number below the line of the floor indicates the advanced foot, and a period the foot which is behind; a comma below the period indicates a ball position, and a very small circle a toe or "point" position. A circle surrounding certain signs of the legs indicates that such positions are assumed during the execution of a *pirouette* or turn. The direction in which the turn is to be made is indicated by the direction of the circular sign, and the turning foot is shown by the sign of position. The thick end shows the starting, and the arrow-head the finishing point of the turn. If the beginning of the circle extends below the line of the floor it indicates a forward turn; if to the right, a right turn. The term "right" applies to the right side of the dancer, who is supposed always to face the spectator unless otherwise stated. The shaded line which is used to show the head represents the hair, and by it one may show the direction of the face, and even of the eyes.

925. In figures so small as those in the example it is difficult to draw them exactly, but the arm-positions can hardly fail to be understood. The 4th position of the feet is generally indicated by the number, and crossed positions of the legs by a little cross (×) above the line of the supporting leg (§ 105).

Execution of the Cachucha

Prelude. Chords.

FIRST COUPLET

MEAS.

-I

926. Figure 1. Ziz-zag Forward (*Ballonné Progressif*). (Sixteen measures.)

Enter from background at left, proceeding diagonally forward to the right, by
  means of three *ballonnés dessous*, one *pirouette* and one *frappé dessus*, into 5th
  position.   4
Repeat obliquely to the left.   4
Repeat obliquely to the right.   4
Repeat obliquely to the left to centre.   4

927. Figure II. (*Pivoter*.) (Sixteen measures.)

Turn slowly backward to the left upon the place by means of six *pas de ciseaux
  dessous*, in 2d and 5th positions with the left arm raised, but without raising upon
  the toe.   6
Pirouette basque to left.   2
Repetition to the right.   8

SYLL.	**928. Figure III. Zig-zag Backward (*Ballonné Rétrograde*).** (Sixteen measures.)	
1–3	One *ballonné* to right, followed by raising into 5th point position and audible lowering of right heel, and carry left foot into 2d position balancing.	I
1	Put down left in 2d position.	
2	Glide right into anterior 5th position, pointing toe strongly downward, and audibly lowering the heel, immediately carrying the left into posterior balancing position.	

SYLL.		MEAS.
3	Carry left foot to 2d position and transfer.	I
	During this measure the right arm executes a large arm-circle (*grand rond de bras*), accompanied by bending the body to such a degree that the right hand nearly touches the floor, and then a corresponding movement of the left arm.	
1	Carry right foot to 2d position and transfer.	
2–3	Execute a *tour entier* upon right ball or point, carrying left foot first into 2d balancing, and thence into anterior 5th point position, and transfer.	I
1	Pound with whole sole of right foot into anterior 5th position, and transfer.	
2	Rest.	
3	Begin the *ballonné* as preparation for the repetition.	I
	Ballonné rétrograde to left.	4
	Repetition of entire *enchaînement*.	8

929. Figure IV. (*Frappé Tortillé.*) In the background. (Sixteen measures.)

Traversée to right sidewise with one *frappé* and one *tortillé* repeated three times, and followed by one *coupé* and one *pas de basque latéral*.

1	One *frappé* with right into 2d position, and transfer.	
2	Turn left foot upon the heel until the toe comes to a point a little in advance of the right heel.	
3	Turn left into anterior 5th sole position.	I
	The second and third syllables constitute a *pas tortillé*.	
1–3	Repetition of first measure.	I
1–3	Repetition of second measure.	I
1	Execute *coupé dessous* with right foot into posterior 5th ball position.	
2	Put down left foot in 2d position, and transfer.	
3	Draw right foot into crossed anterior 4-5 position, and transfer.	I

41

SYLL.		MEAS.
	The second and third syllables of the preceding measure constitute the *pas de basque espagnol*.	
	Repeat preceding four measures to left.	4
	Repeat preceding four measures to right.	4
	Two *frappés tortillés*.	2
	Coupé pas de basque.	1
1	*Frappé* on right foot into anterior 4th position, and transfer.	
2	Rest.	
3	Preparatory movement for succeeding *pas ballonné*.	1

SECOND COUPLET

930. Figure 1. The Inclined Rhombus Forward (*Le Rhombe en Descendant*).

Obliquely forward to right to the middle line by one and a half *ballonnés*, two *pas élevés* forward into 4th position, one *demi-pas de basque* to left, one *tappé du talon gauche* (stamp with left heel), and one *frappé* with right into 2d position.

931. Divide figure into periods of several syllables. It is of advantage to both instructor and pupil to treat this figure as a verse-line divided into eleven syllables or counts, which may be designated as follows:

0̆, 1̄ 2 3̆, 4̄ 5̆ 6̆, 7̄ 8 9̆, and 1̄0.

0 During the first part-measure, hop upon the left foot, carrying the right foot forward into balancing position and raising right arm to correspond, which is nearly to 5th position, and following the movement by lifting the eyes to the upstretched hand.

1 Upon the first syllable of the first measure, put down right foot in 2d position, and transfer.

SYLL.		MEAS.

2   Draw left foot into posterior 3d heel position, and transfer.

These three syllables constitute a ball step, or *pas ballonné* [§ 527].

3–4   Repeat first two syllables of *pas ballonné*.

5–6   Execute two high *pas élevés* upon line of direction.

7   Carry left foot into 2d position, and transfer.

8   Swing right foot into crossed anterior 4–5 position.

Syllables seven and eight constitute a half basque step or *demi-pas de basque*.

932.   The name *demi-pas de basque* is entirely correct, for in executing it one steps half to the side and carries the other foot into crossed balancing position, but does not transfer the weight.

933.   The step is called *pointe de pied* by many Spanish dancers, but that term is too indefinite, as it does not in any way explain the manner in which it should be done.

9   Raise left heel and lower it audibly, with weight still resting upon it. This movement is known as stamping or *taper* (§ 265).

10   Stamp with right foot into 2d position and transfer, and rest during the second syllable of the fourth measure, again resuming the dance upon the third syllable thereof, by preparation for the succeeding step.

Most of the step-sentences of the *Cachucha* and other Spanish dances may be analyzed in the above manner.

The same *enchaînement* is repeated upon the next four measures with the other foot, and extends obliquely forward to the centre line of the stage. The accompanying arm-movements are clearly shown in the choregraphic description.   4

The same *enchaînement* is again performed upon the next four measures, commencing with the right foot and going backward obliquely to the left as far as the horizontal middle line of the stage. In doing this, it is necessary for the dancer to nearly turn her back to the spectators.   4

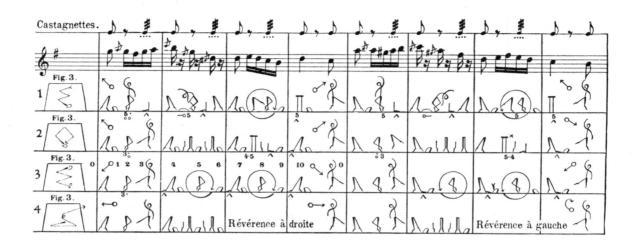

SYLL.		MEAS.
	Still another repetition of this combination upon the remaining four measures brings the dancer once more to her place in the centre of the background, where, by means of the *demi-pas de basque*, she again faces the spectators.	4

Figure II.

This figure, which consists of sixteen *demi-pas de basque*, with *tapés de talon*, brings the dancer to the front of the stage, as shown in the script.

16

Figure III. The Inclined Rhombus Backward (*Le Rhombe en Montant*).

This figure is exactly similar to the first figure of the Couplet, except that it is in counter-motion.

16

934. Figure IV. In the foreground.

Demi-traversée à droite, consisting of *coupé-tortillé, coupé-pas de basque, frappé-ramassé* and *frappé-pirouette*.

4

The steps have already been explained in their respective places in this Grammar; but the following repetition of the explanations is given that the reader may more readily understand their application in this dance. For that reason the *enchainement* has been divided into twelve syllables, in the same manner as previously employed.

1	*Coupé.* Put down left foot forcibly in posterior 5th position, and transfer.	
2	*Tortillé.* Turn right foot inward upon the ball.	
3	Turn right foot outward into anterior 5th position, and transfer.	
4	*Coupé.* Put down left foot forcibly in posterior 5th ball position, and transfer, thus releasing right.	
5	*Pas de basque.* Carry right to 2d position, and transfer.	

44

Révérence au partèrre et sortie par des pas ballonnés

SYLL.		MEAS.
6	Carry left, by a circular movement, into anterior crossed 4-5 position, and transfer.	
7	*Frappé.* Stamp with right into 2d position, and transfer.	
8	*Ramassé.* Bend supporting right leg, and glide left foot into anterior 5th point position with corresponding bending of left leg, simultaneously bending the body and dipping the left arm to such a degree that it would be possible to pick up with the left hand a small object lying upon the floor. The movement receives its name from this bending, and the meaning of the word *ramasser* is to pick up.	
	The right arm is raised during this movement to a corresponding position in the opposite direction, and the eyes follow the movement of the left hand.	
9	Put down left and raise right heel, and straighten the body, commencing thereby the transfer of weight, which is completed upon syllable	
10	by a stamp in 2d position with the right foot.	
11	Raise right heel and execute a complete turn to right upon the toe, with left leg in three-quarters high flowing 2d position.	
12	Put down left foot in 2d position, and transfer.	
	Retraversée to left with same *enchaînement*, but in counter-motion.	4
	Repeat to right.	4
	Repeat to left to centre, but without *ramassé*.	4

THIRD COUPLET

Figure I. Zig-Zag Backward (*Ballonné Rétrograde*).

Same as third figure of first couplet. — 16

Figure II. In the background upon the place.

Three *temps de ciseaux*, without hopping or turning, one *coupé* and one *pas de basque* to the right. — 4

45

SYLL.		MEAS.

Repeat. — 4

Pivoter to left, with left arm raised and *pirouette basque* to left, as in the second figure of the first couplet. — 8

Figure III.

Zig-Zag forward, with two successive *pirouettes*. *Enchaînement* of ten syllables.

SYLL.		MEAS.
0	Hop preparatory to *pas ballonné*.	
1–4	Move obliquely forward to the right half-way to centre, by one and a half *pas ballonnés*.	
5	Complete turn upon right ball with left foot in balancing anterior 5th position with perpendicular sole.	
6	Put down left into anterior 5th sole position, and transfer.	
7	Stamp with right into 2d position, and transfer.	
8–9	Repeat turning as in fifth and sixth syllables.	
10	Stamp with right into 2d position, and transfer.	
	Repeat *enchaînement* to left.	4
	Repeat figure.	8

935. Figure IV. *Ramassé*. (Sixteen measures.)

Short zig-zag to rear with eight raising and picking up movements.

The phrase contains six syllables.

Execution :

Preparation : *Temps-levé* (this consists of a *fouetté* and a hop preparatory to the *pas ballonné*).

SYLL.	
1	Put down right foot in 2d position, and transfer.
2	*Ramassé* (already explained).
3	Put down left and raise right heel.

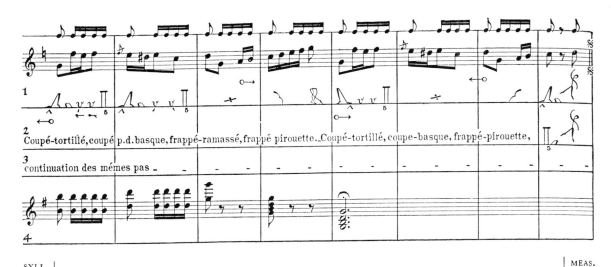

SYLL.		MEAS.
4	Stamp with right into 2d position.	
5	*Temps fouetté-dessous.* Under crossed whip-syllable. (See § 487 *et seq.*)	
6	*Temps levé*, as used in the part-measure as preparation for *pas ballonné*.	
	This *enchainement* of six syllables is danced alternately eight times, and brings the dancer at its end into the centre of the background.	16

FOURTH COUPLET

936. Figure 1. *Grand Dégagé.*

Execution: Zig-zag forward to right and left, to a point slightly in front of the horizontal middle line of the stage.

The enchainment contains ten syllables.

o	Part-measure. Movement preparatory for *pas ballonné*.	
1–4	Move obliquely forward to right, half-way to centre, by means of one and a half *pas ballonnés*.	
5–6	Slowly execute one and a quarter turns upon the right toe, with left foot in high balancing 2d position.	
7	Put down left foot in anterior 4th position, raising the left arm and following its movement with the eyes.	
8	Transfer slowly and with dignity to left foot, at the same time bending the upper body, lowering the left and raising the right arm and bending the knees.	
9	Transfer, in like manner, to right foot.	
10	Raise again as in seventh syllable.	
	The dancer rests upon the eleventh syllable, and upon the twelfth executes again the movement preparatory to the repetition of the *enchainement* in the other direction.	4

47

The music should be rendered *rallentando* from the fifth to the tenth syllable. MEAS.

These movements should all be executed in an easy, airy manner, with corresponding arm movements.

Repeat to the left forward to horizontal middle line. 4

Repeat to the right forward half way to front. 4

Repeat to left forward to a point slightly beyond the middle line of the front, kneeling slowly upon the left knee during the sixteenth measure, with right arm lowered and left arm raised, head slightly inclined forward, and eyes downcast. 4

937. Figure II. Transfer upon the Knees (*Dégagé à Genoux*).

During the first four measures, carry the right arm inside the right leg, by a *grand rond de bras*, which proceeds thence upward and through a raised position, returning again to a lowered attitude outside the right leg, accompanied by a similar but opposite movement of the left arm. During all this the eyes follow the movement of the right hand, while the head and body involuntarily coöperate. 4

During the fifth measure, carry the left arm into the crossed anterior horizontal position, and turn the upper body slightly to the left, following with the eyes the movement of the left hand, and rise slowly during the sixth measure, upon the right foot, at the same time continuing the raising of the body and the movements of the arms.

During the seventh measure, carry the right foot into 2d position, and transfer, and execute with the left a *jeté en tournant*, sinking in the eighth measure upon the right knee. 4

Repeat the entire *enchaînement* in counter-motion to the eighth measure, in which the dancer, instead of kneeling as before, pauses during two syllables in anterior 5th position of right, once more executing upon the third syllable the movement preparatory to the *pas ballonné*. 8

938. Figure III. In the foreground.

One and a half *pas ballonnés* and two *pas élevés* to the right. 2

Deep curtesy to right, directed particularly to the occupants of the corresponding boxes, to whom the eyes are turned. 2
4

Repetition of *enchaînement* to left.

Backward to centre by two and a half *pas ballonnés* in circular direction to right, followed by complete turn to right upon right toe, and low curtesy to centre to spectators. 8

CODA

The dancer concludes with one and a half *pas ballonnés* and several *pas élevés* to left. Exit left upon last syllable of music.

APPENDIX A

The Cachucha

Problems Met and Adjustments Made

IN HIS BOOK "The Grammar of the Art of Dancing" Zorn gives the choreography of the dance in his system of notation and also describes it in word notes. Neither is complete. Fortunately where the one is abbreviated or unclear, the other provides some missing information. Words and notation do not always agree, so movement logic based on relation to the music became the deciding factor. How far can the stick figures be taken literally? Are slight variations in arm positions intended or are they slips of the writer's hand? The tiny feet on the stick figures are clear, but are they exact? Zorn's publication lacked a good proof reader.

Timing: Zorn placed the stick figures under the music notes to indicate timing. This cannot be followed religiously, one has to make adjustments to produce kinetic sense. Timing given in the word notes often differs from the notation. The words seem to be more reliable.

1. *Introduction*

In the Zorn notation two chords of music are given as an introduction, following which the dancer enters from offstage with the first Ballonné Progressif step. The sheet music gives two versions: 'Introduction a.' of four measures, and 'Introduction b.', the two chords given by Zorn. John Lanchbery combined a. and b. to make the longer introduction used by Ballet For All. During this, the dancer enters and takes the pose made famous by the lithograph of Fanny Elssler.

A preparatory port de bras and épaulement have been added for this version.

2. *Level of Steps*

What is the level for steps? Most of the tiny figure drawings show the dancer to be on ¾ toe. The whole foot support occurs only in the closing in 5th (meas. 4, etc.), or when the heel is lowered to make an accent (meas. 57, etc.). Is this preponderance of ½ or ¾ toe intended? Nothing in the word notes suggests this. On occasion the figure is shown with the sign for pointe: "o" clearly stated for the support (meas. 33 ct. 2; 137 ct. 2; 141 ct. 2; 203 ct. 1). This is also mentioned in the word notes for meas. 35, 116, and 194, in which execution of a full turn on the right toe is stated. It can only be concluded that, whereas for touching gestures 'toe' meant the tip of the toe, for supports it meant the ¾ pointe.

3. Transference of Weight

Unlike many systems of notation, Zorn has a specific indication for transference of weight. He tends to indicate the leg gesture which precedes the transference as well as the transference itself. Perhaps it is lack of good proof reading that has resulted in certain inconsistencies and in absence of logic in the use of the weight transference sign. At the end of meas. 67 the weight is shown to transfer to the right (⌒). At the start of 68 it transfers again to the right. This also happens in 71 and 72. At other times a step or a landing is missing. In meas. 145 the figure ⟋⟍ should be ⟋⟍ and so on.

4. Stamps

Accents for stamps are omitted in several places. Meas. 71, count 1, has no accent, as is stated in 67. No doubt Zorn became lazy and only gave partial notation in some places (a temptation we understand only too well!).

Zorn often shows a stamp as a gesture, a separate shift of weight onto that foot following after. The stamp of meas. 49 is illustrated in Ex. 4a) and b). All such indications were translated as Ex. 4c), a stamping step (support). As a stamping gesture, 4b), the action suggests fly swatting which is surely not intended. The stamp in 2nd which ends each phrase of the Rhombe en Descendant is most awkwardly depicted in the Zorn figures. In meas. 68 both feet appear to be on pointe; in meas. 72 the stamp is indicated as a whole foot contact, but as a gesture, with the supporting foot on ¾ toe, Ex. 4d) and e), a most awkward position.

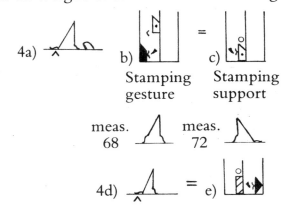

5. Cou-de-Pied

Every Zorn cou-de-pied position is shown as 5a) with the foot vertically down, even for pirouettes. This has been given in the score as b). It is not clear whether all cou-de-pied positions were done in that manner at that period. It is certainly a stylistic difference which requires some practice.

6. Arms

Throughout the Zorn notation arms are very static. As a typical example, in meas. 1-4, the arms remain in the same position until the repeat to the other side. No transition for the arms is given and no change for the arms for the pirouette (meas. 3), nor for the pose after the pirouette (meas. 4). We do not believe that Fanny danced this way and so ports de bras were added where they seemed appropriate.

7. *Turning, Pirouettes*

The direction of turning in Zorn notation easily confuses the unwary. In Zorn the arrows of a) and b) are visually both clockwise, whereas the turning direction of c) and d) appear to be anti-clockwise. The instructions in the book state that 7a) is clockwise on the right foot, and b) anticlockwise on the right foot, as indicated here. Ex. c) and d) follow the same logic. For meas. 17-23, the direction of turning in Zorn's notation is not com-

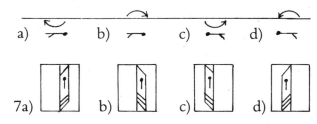

pletely clear. The word notes say turn left, the stage plan diagram illustrates turning right. If the stage plan is in fact a notation indication and not a stage plan, then, following the above code, it would be turning to the left. The change in meaning of the arrows according to whether one is on the right or left foot is indeed confusing.

8. *The Ballonné Step*

In the Zorn book (p. 146, para. 527) the description for a ballonné, the "Ball Step" is given thus: "This step derives its name from the circular movement of the free foot, which has the appearance of stepping over a ball. It is usually executed to the side, but it may also be made forward or backward. Although it may be practised alternately, it is usually applied in 'simple' form, that is, without any change of direction." Execution of the Ball Step is given as follows:

"Preparation: 3d or 5th position of right. The first syllable commences in the part measure, with a jump★ on the left foot, during which the right is carried in a circular direction to the 2d position, where it immediately receives the weight. In the second syllable, the left foot glides into posterior 5th position. In order to maintain the same direction, it is necessary to add a transfer to the second syllable, but such is not necessary in the case of alternate ball steps."

In the examples below, 8a) illustrates the verbal description, 8b) the figure drawings which accompany the verbal description, and 8c) the transcription of the ballonné as it appears in the actual dance. To achieve the curved design, it is written in Labanotation as 8d) (see Glossary). For ballet trained dancers it is difficult to achieve the curved design, the ballonné tends to be performed as 8e) which produces an angular air design.

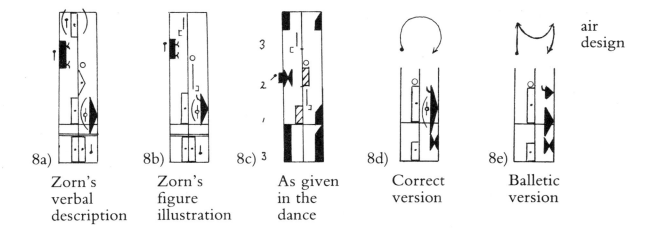

8a)	8b)	8c)	8d)	8e)
Zorn's verbal description	Zorn's figure illustration	As given in the dance	Correct version	Balletic version

★a hop is meant, of course.

9. Pivoter (meas. 17-32)

In the Pivoter, the foot touching behind in 5th on ct. 3 is shown by Zorn to be on pointe with a flexed ankle. This position happens more naturally if a ball of the foot touch is used. The artificiality of use of the pointe with a flexed ankle seemed unlikely, hence this was not followed.

The word description states six pas de ciseaux, the notation gives repeats for seven. Six were chosen to allow more time for the 'Pirouette Basque', for which artistic licence was introduced in the addition of the back bend.

10. Ballonné Retrograde (meas. 33-35)

To follow the floor plan the dancer must travel. The original notation indicates the directional supports of Ex. 10c). This results in the performer staying on the same spot, therefore adjustments were made, such as use of Ex. a) instead of b), to provide the required travelling. Several adjustments had to be made to make all possible steps travel.

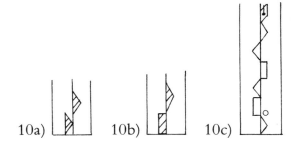

Timing of the Ballonné Retrograde
More material is contained in this step than can comfortably fit into the time available. Hence the alternate version to allow the dancer to find the timing which is comfortable to her.

11. Frappé Tortillé (meas. 52)

For the pas de basque in this step we changed the rhythm slightly, making it uneven to provide a lilt and to highlight the port de bras in preparation for the arm change.

12. Transition to Le Rhombe (meas. 64)

The word notes give a coupé under on count 2 which will produce a rather hurried ballonné preparation for meas. 65. We left count 1 as a stamping gesture and took the ballonné from there. 12a) is the original, b) is our version.

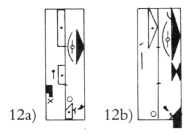

13. Le Rhombe en Descendant (meas. 65)

The word notes and notation disagree on the counts given. For the ♩ upbeat, the words state: "hop upon the left foot, . . . Upon the first syllable of the first measure, put down right foot in 2d position, and transfer." Zorn's notation shows Ex. 13a) for the upbeat, landing on the left foot on count 1, and transferring the weight on the 'and' of count 1. We followed the word notes.

Another inconsistency which occurs in the Rhombe step, is the closing into 5th on meas. 69. This instance of 5th position is the odd man out since in all other instances closing into 3rd is used.

The directions described for the steps do not facilitate producing the desired floor plan. Ex. 13b) is a translation of the word description. The Zorn notation is also not helpful here.

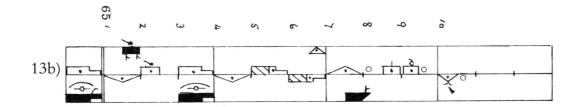

13b)

The stage direction faced for the Rhombe, effacé or écarté, is not clear. In the 1967 version all travelling was interpreted as being directly forward, as in Ex. 13c). In 1980, for the film we chose the alignment which best related to the audience, hence the more complex appearance of the Labanotation for this section. Some indication of use of head had been given, but this will be somewhat individual to each performer.

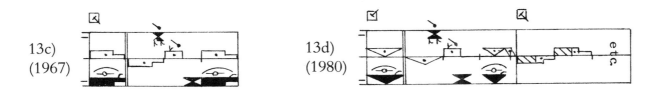

13c)
(1967)

13d)
(1980)

14. *Le Rhombe (meas. 67 and 71)*

The notation for these measures is rather confusing. In the Zorn notation the movement was spelled out as 14a). The stamp was given as a gesture touching the floor with the toe, with the transference of weight occuring afterwards. This I translated as an immediate support, Ex. 14b), changing the side direction to 〉 to follow more closely the line of travel. After the heel drop on ct. 3, Zorn shows the weight to transfer to the right (⌒). The right toe then "stamps" before the weight is transferred to the right. This repeated weight transference occurs on 70/71, and also 75/76 and 79/80. Movement logic and the word notes dictated the rendition of Ex. 14b).

In meas. 75 and 79 the pattern in Zorn's notation is similar to meas. 67 and 71 but abbreviated. I decided that all were intended to be the same; Zorn was obviously shortcutting the notation.

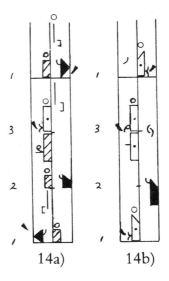

14a)   14b)

15. *Arm Gestures (meas. 67, 71, etc.)*

As no arm movements were indicated, traditional gestures in Spanish dance, derived from the Panaderos, were added to this step pattern.

16. *Timing of Le Rhombe en Descendant*

This step contains two delightful features which are not shown to advantage at the speed established. In the alternate version the stamp at the end is eliminated to give more fullness to the charming pas élevés and the demi-pas de basque tapé with its accompanying curved outstretching arm gesture. As so many of the step patterns end with a stamp and a pause on the fourth measure, a change in this ending seemed a welcome variation, and defensible artistic licence.

17. *Demi-Pas de Basque (meas. 81)*

Repetition of the 16 demi-pas de basque with identical arm movement seemed unlikely, hence artistic licence was taken here in varying the arm pattern. In meas. 96 the transition into the next section seemed hurried, therefore the last pas de basque was cut short, allowing time for the ballonné. This placed the next phrase on a more clear-cut beat.

18. *Tortillé, Pas de Basque (meas. 113)*

The original states the arms as Ex. 18a). This was changed to b) for the following reasons:

18a) and 18b) [notation symbols]

It is likely that the eyes will be looking at the right foot during the tortillé, and as a result the body will bend slightly toward that foot. Therefore it is better for the right arm to be low, as in b). For the arm movement which follows in the ramassé, the left arm must be low, near the floor. In the original version the arm is already low and hence has little movement. By starting with the left arm up, a larger sweeping movement can be made.

19. *Ballonné Pirouettes (meas. 161)*

To bring more variety and attack for the pirouettes, the ballonnés here were modified into the "contemporary" ballonné form, ending on the cou-de-pied. Also to avoid the awkward timing of meas. 161, placement of the movement sequence in relation to the music was adjusted. In meas. 164 the arm transition, chest twist and head movement have been added.

20. *Temps Levé Ramassé (meas. 176, 177, 178)*

The original of this in the Zorn notation is most awkward. To solve it the ballonné preparation before the step to the right on count 1 of bar 177 was deleted. Because in the music counts 2 and 3 of meas. 176 are silent, there is no music cue to accompany the movement. Also it is difficult to fit the ballonné in (the spring and the landing) and then to step to the right on count 1, meas. 177. A turn on count 3 of meas. 176 was added to start the repeat of the pattern in the right direction.

21. *Grand Dégagé*

Meas. 193 Neither notation nor word notes are clear for this step. Because the verbal instructions say "Slowly execute one and a quarter turns . . ." one feels that more time should be given to the turn in 2nd, a highlight of this step. Therefore in the alternate version the ballonné has been placed a beat earlier and only one ballonné performed instead of two. Note that the "modern" ballonné has again been used here, to provide impetus ('attack'), leading into the turn.

Meas. 195. The words say "Transfer slowly and with dignity to the left foot . . ." There is not time for this even when the music is retarded. How exactly should the port de bras be performed? Neither words nor notation give a clear indication. Three versions of the arm movements are given in Labanotation. The standard version in the score is a windmill pattern, the left arm ending up. Zorn shows the supports to end in a high 4th position, with the body upright. This pose seemed uncharacteristic, so a slight backward arch of the chest was added. In Alternate Versions A and B the support is lower and the bend deeper. Alternate Version A provides a circular arm pattern ending with the left arm in line with the backbend. This version was used in the film. At the end of the windmill arm pattern of Alternate Version B, the gaze to the audience is through the curve of the arm.

22. *Dégagé à Genoux*

Meas. 208, etc. The facing direction is not clear. The notation suggests ⊞, but the floor plan shows ⌷ which means face ⊡ but do not travel. We decided that ⌺ would produce a better line.

Meas. 209-213. Zorn's word notes for the grand rond de bras are not clear, nor is the notation. Meas. 212 and 213 are identical in the notation, suggesting that there is no movement. The word notes indicate continuous movement, but one questions correctness of the eyes following the "right hand" when the direction of the grand rond de bras suggests the eyes should follow the left hand. Similarly "During the fifth measure, carry the left arm . . ." only makes sense if it is the right arm, and again "following with the eyes the movement of the left hand," would make more sense if it is the right.

   Interpretation of this section has been of a large sweeping Grand Port de Bras typical of Spanish dance with full use of torso bending and twisting.

23. *Ballonnés, Pas Élevés*

Meas. 227. In the Ballet For All production a rose was thrown to the dancer at stage left. This she throws over her shoulder as she exits. In the original ballet in which the Cachucha appeared, Elssler is thrown a rose. She is depicted with a rose in one of the lithographs, hence the rose was introduced in the film.

24. *Examples of Translations of the Steps*

The first literal translation of Zorn's notation into Labanotation was later worked into fluent, kinetic dance "language." Below are two typical examples.

   Note that Zorn's indication of transference of weight: ⌒ is translated as: ⊔ since no level or direction is stated, the direction being where the foot touched previously.

Ballonné Progressif

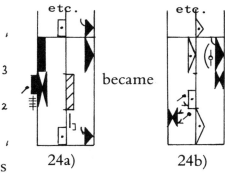

became

Most of the adjustments were based on the word notes which supplied many needed clues in making the movement sequences logical and flowing.

24a)   24b)

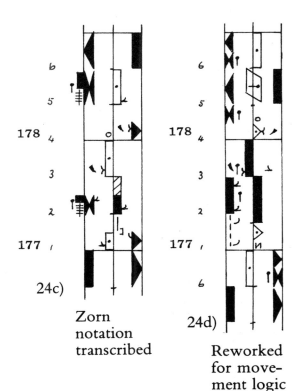

24c)

Zorn notation transcribed

24d)

Reworked for movement logic

55

Friedrich Albert Zorn
A Biographical Note

by IVOR GUEST

FRIEDRICH ALBERT ZORN was born in 1815, the son of a dancing master called Jacob Zorn. Early in life he acquired an irresistible taste for travel. He left home at the age of sixteen, and for a few years led a restless, peripatetic existence. In 1835 he was teaching in Dresden, and the following year he moved to Christiana (now Oslo). He was soon on the move again, having decided to invest his hard-earned savings in a visit to Paris to broaden his knowledge and gain experience, and then it was that he must have seen, and like everyone else been overwhelmed by, Fanny Elssler's performance of the *Cachucha*. In December 1837 he returned to Germany, where he had no sooner settled down to teach dancing and gymnastics when the urge to travel came over him again and he set off with the intention of discovering the riches of European folk dance. At length, in March 1839, he reached Odessa, which he found so much to his taste that he decided to settle there. A year later he was engaged as teacher of dancing at the Richelieu Gymnasium, a post he was to hold for the remainder of his active life, a span of some fifty years.

Remote though Odessa was from the main centres of European civilisation, Albert Zorn was able to keep abreast of the latest developments in his art. Being of an intellectual and studious nature, he became fascinated by the subject of dance notation and entered into an extensive correspondence with Arthur Saint-Léon, who had invented an ingenious method that was considerably in advance of anything that had been devised before. The elements of this method, known as *Sténochorégraphie,* were set out in a manual which Saint-Léon himself published in 1852. Zorn subscribed to this publication when it originally came out in parts, and began using the method which, in his own words, he "amplified and perfected."

Zorn continued to travel widely and maintained contact with many prominent teachers and choreographers, one of his trips – in 1855 – being to Berlin for discussions with Paul Taglioni. He became a member of the Academy of German Dance Teachers (Akademie der Deutsche Tanzlehrkunst) which was formed in 1873, finding among its members a number of kindred spirits who shared his views on the necessity of developing a universal method of recording dance movement. One of these was Bernhard Klemm of Leipzig, who had himself invented a relatively unsophisticated notation system which he had described in his book *Katechismus der Tanzkunst,* published in 1855.

Zorn's "Grammar", which was conceived both as a teacher's manual of dance technique and a textbook of his notation system, took shape over a long period of gestation. Among his colleagues who helped him in its preparation were A. Freising, who taught dancing at the Royal University in Berlin, and Otto Stoige, ballet-master in Königsberg. Indeed it was thanks to the influence of Freising, who was President of the Academy of German Dance Teachers, that the Grammar was commended in the 1885 report to the members of the Academy. The work was eventually published by J. J. Weber in Leipzig in 1887 under the title *Grammatik der Tanzkunst: theoretischer und praktischer Unterricht in der Tanzkunst und Tanzschreibkunst oder Choregraphie*. It was adopted by the Academy as a textbook, and a resolution was passed at the annual meeting that each member should procure a copy and send in his comments, with the intention of publishing these suggestions in a supplement or incorporating them in a later edition.

The next edition was in fact the Russian edition, published in 1889 and 1890, in a translation by F. N. Anderson. In a preface Zorn was at pains to point out that this was "by no means a mere translation of the German edition of the manual; it is a completely new edition of my work, which has been extensively rewritten and considerably augmented and corrected." On the title page of this edition Zorn was named, after the Russian fashion, as Albert Yakovlevich Zorn, and a notice added the information that he had published other works, one of these a Russian folk dance for two persons, *Vozle rechki, vozle mosta* (By the river, by the bridge), containing precise descriptions in Russian, German and French, music arranged for piano, and dance notation added under the music staves; another, two Hungarian dances, *Kër* and a *Hungarian Waltz*. The original German edition of the manual was also advertised, with the recommendation that it had been "very flatteringly received by the Russian, German, American and even South African press."

These publications were to be obtained from bookshops and music shops, and also from the author at his home at No. 13 Gretcheskaya Street, Odessa. At this address Albert Zorn was still giving lessons in 1890, assisted now by his nephew L. E. Prauss, and an advertisement in the *Odessa News* announced that he was available to visit educational institutions and private homes.

With the publication of his book Zorn became a revered and respected figure in the world of dance teaching, and in 1893 was invited to Boston to take the chair at the second Congress of Dancing (the first having been held two years before). Apparently he did not attend the third Congress in Berlin in 1894, but his influence was still strong for, according to G. Desrat (in his *Dictionnaire de la Danse*, 1895), at the final session "a long-studied question took a great step forward, that of a uniform terminology and notation for the dance, as there is in music. The Grammar of the teacher from Odessa naturally won everyone's vote, and no doubt remains the bedrock of choreography." The work of these Congresses, which were concerned with social dancing, has so far received little attention from modern researchers and historians.

Zorn's Grammar seems to have been published for the first time in English during the year of the Boston Congress. According to Desrat it was published under the direction of E. Woodworth Masters, a well-known Boston teacher who organised the American National Association of Masters of Dancing of the United States and Canada and was its first President from 1883 to 1893, and an announcement in the periodical *The Galop* of June 1893 stated that it was "now fully printed and ready for delivery in book form, 351 pages, paper covers, price $3.00." Two years later the Atlas volume followed, translated by Karl Klein of the University of Halle. So far, however, no copy of this edition has come to light.

The date of Zorn's death has not been recorded, but he had probably died by the time the second edition of his book, edited by Alfonso Josephs Sheafe,* was published in 1905. This edition, dedicated to the American National Association of Masters of Dancing of the United States and Canada, was presumably based on the earlier edition put out by Woodworth Masters.

---

*It is a curious coincidence that Alfonso J. Sheafe was a distant relative of Ann Hutchinson, her grandmother having been a Sheafe.

APPENDIX C

Notes on

The Film of Fanny Elssler's Cachucha

THE FILM of the Cachucha, danced by Margaret Barbieri, principal dancer of the Sadler's Wells Royal Ballet, illustrates a performance of the work by a gifted, sensitive artiste.

Although the film was made for educational purposes, it was important that it be a *performance* of the work rather than a 'recitation' of precisely how each step should be performed. Thus Barbieri was given freedom for her own interpretation of the material. In some instances this meant a slight departure from the script, but repeated rehearsing for precision would have killed the spontaneity and personal expression. Because precise detail exists in the notation, there is no need for such accuracy in a live performance. To undertake a detailed study of the work, whether for research or performance, each student will turn to the score, as in the case of music or drama.

In rehearsing the work for the film, choices existed between alternate versions when the original notation was not quite clear. In addition, decisions had to be made as to how best to perform the steps at the established tempi of the music. In all historical reconstructions, determining the appropriate speed for the accompanying music is a real problem since there is no way of knowing how slow is 'slow', nor how fast is 'fast'. In arranging and rehearsing the music, John Lanchbery felt it essential to keep it bright and lively and so did not allow a slower pace, which, in several instances would have suited the dance steps better. On the other hand, we know from experience that in the process of notating, the writer often tends to slow the steps down, thus squeezing out more detail than can be fully performed at speed. Thus, in the Cachucha, full performance of all the detail given in the notation has not always been possible. Certain aspects had to be skimmed over or, in one instance, repetition of part of a step eliminated to avoid the phrase being too rushed.

For her own artistic interpretation of the dance Margaret Barbieri made her own choices concerning the alternate versions. The versions of the steps which she did not use in the dance itself are illustrated separately in the film. In the Labanotation score the 'standard' version is given in the score itself and the alternate versions in a separate section. In the film the following choices were made:

Ballonné Rétrograde – Barbieri performed the alternate version.

The Rhombes en Descendant and en Montant – the standard version was used.

Grand Dégagé – the alternate version was used in which the arms perform the circular pattern.

In the film the dance is presented first in its entirety, shot from a stationary camera showing the whole of the dance area. Alternate versions of certain steps are then demonstrated, followed by a repeat of the entire dance filmed with the camera following the dancer at a closer range. This provides a clearer view of the movement expression but the sense of stage pattern is lost. However, as the floor plans are clearly set forth in the notation, there is no need to rely on the film for this information.

The film was designed to be a companion piece to this publication and is available for hire and for purchase. Further details can be obtained from Dr. Ann Hutchinson Guest, Language of Dance Centre, 17 Holland Park, London W11 3TD.

Discography

"The Magic of Dance" by Margot Fonteyn: Royal Opera House Orchestra, conducted by Ashley Lawrence. (BBC records, REP 363).

 This record contains an orchestrated version of the Cachucha music. It omits one whole couplet, and therefore, to use it for classroom purposes, the following adjustments need to be made in the dance score:

Section I (meas. 1-64): perform as written.
Sections II and III are combined into one section, here called 'A'.

A1 – Ballonné Pirouette
 (III 3, meas. 161-176)
A2 – Ramassé (III 4, meas. 177-192)
A3 – Rhombe en Descendant
 (II 1, meas. 65-80)
A4 – Coupé Tortillé (II 4, meas. 113-128)

Section IV (meas. 193 to end): perform as written.

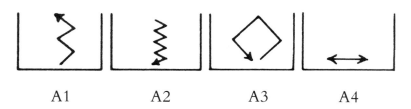

The floor plans for this arrangement.